Superkay and Rocky VS. Big Baby

By Witty Lovett

All Rights Reserved. No part of this publication may be reproduced in any form or by any means, including scanning, photocopying, or otherwise without prior written permission of the copyright holder. Copyright © 2015

Superkay and Rocky VS. Big Baby

Rehearsals were cut short and everyone rushed inside to get out of the rain. "Field Day will begin tomorrow and I wish you all the best" said Kay's third grade teacher Mrs. Bowling. "A storm is headed this way so everyone have a safe trip home." Kay hated storms especially since she had such a long walk home. While riding home on the school bus, Kay thought about her dog Rocky who met her faithfully at the bus stop even in the rain. As the school bus came to her stop, Kay saw her faithful dog, Rocky, waiting in the pouring rain. He began to bark loudly as if to say hello. Kay stepped off the bus right into a big puddle of water just as the thunder clapped. "Let's run home Rocky!" she yelled. Her feet were soaked and water rained into her eyes as Rocky ran ahead as if he were racing her home, barking all the way. Coming upon a pond, Rocky stopped to look at something that caught his eye. "Keep running Rocky!" Kay shouted. "Rocky did you hear me, keep running!" Now she was close enough to see an old bone by the pond that had gotten his attention. Suddenly thunder clapped again and with a flash of lightning, bright enough to light up the city, Kay and Rocky were both struck, knocking them out.

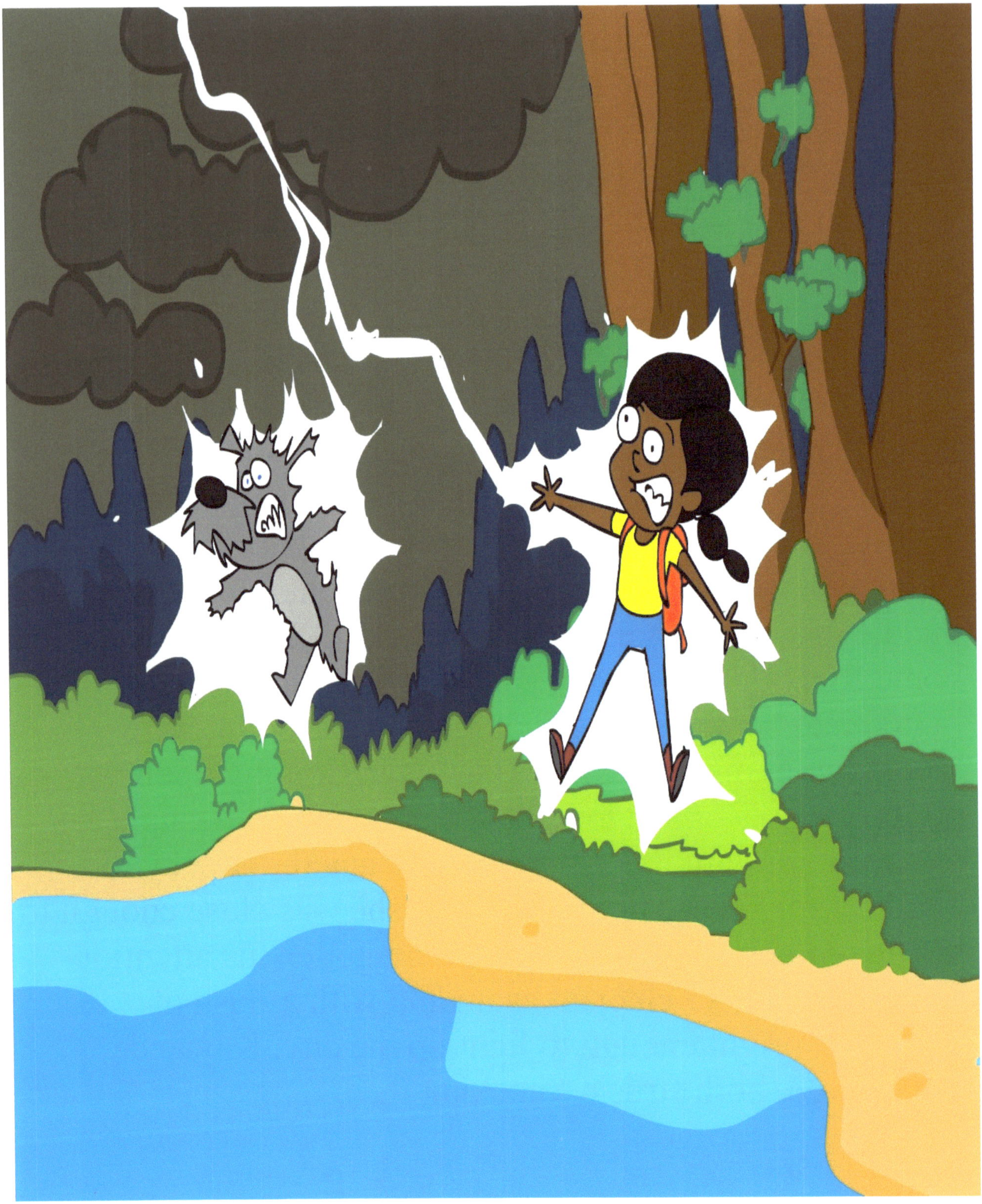

Five minutes later, Kay slowly started to revive and looking around, still shaken from the blast, tried to gather her thoughts. Then she remembered Rocky. She called out "Rocky! Rocky where are you boy?" as she slowly got to her feet. "I'm a-l-i-v-e!" she shouted and leaped into the air to celebrate and didn't come down! "Whoa, what's going on?" she wondered. "I'm flying!" she said. Then noticed her bag was gone and she was now wearing a cape. Although it frightened her a little, it was still pretty cool. Now soaring with her new found powers, she frantically searched for Rocky. "Rocky!" she yelled. "I'm over here" a scruffy voice said. Kay turned around in midair and was amazed to see her faithful companion soaring in front of her eyes wearing a short red cape where his collar used to be. "Didn't recognize me huh? Must be the flying." Rocky said. "Rocky you're talking!" Kay shouted. "Don't forget flying" he joked as he did a loop in midair. "That lightning blast must have caused this change in us" Kay said. "What could this mean?" she continued. "It means I can do this!" Rocky said as he yelled "ZOOM!" doing another loop in the air. "This means we now have super powers" Kay explained. "Super powers?" Rocky asked. "Yes super p-o-w-e-r-s just like all the great heroes" she said.

As Kay was speaking there was a call for help from many miles away. "Help, help somebody please!" a voice cried. Without delay Superkay and her side kick Rocky were on the way. Following the sound for help using their newly acquired super hearing, they arrived on the scene. An elderly man was being robbed. "Hey you down there, leave him alone" Kay yelled. "Who said that?" asked the would-be robber. "Let me get him!" Rocky asked. "No Rocky. This could be dangerous and we're still new at this. I'll make the first move to get him." Kay turned her attention to the robber. She stared at his feet and heat rays began to come from her eyes the heat rays were so intense that they started burning through the robber's shoes causing him to dance and jump around like a jumping bean! He was immediately arrested and the officers removed his hot shoes which were still smoking from the heat. The elderly man turned to ask "how can I ever thank you?" but Superkay and Rocky were already flying home with lightning speed. As Kay entered the house her mom asked "where have you been? They're interviewing your dad on the news broadcast." She followed her mother's gaze as she looked at the television and heard the reporter saying "Mayor, can you tell us what happened?" "The details are sketchy at this point, however, we do have some witnesses" her dad said. "Yes, yes it's true! The duo saved my life savings!" the elderly man exclaimed.

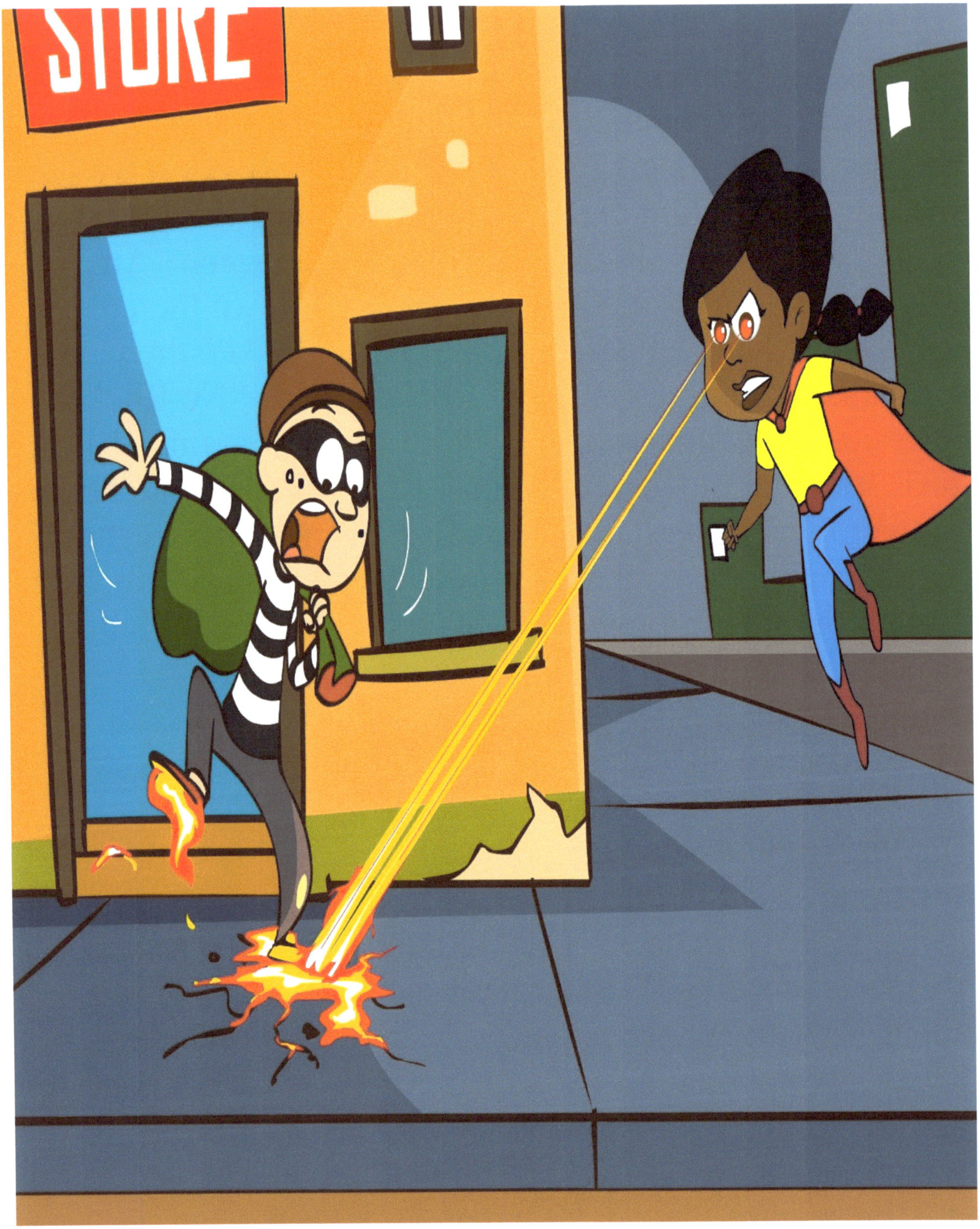
STORE

Superkay and Rocky were talking softly in her room before bed. "I am nine years old and you are a dog but we can make a difference. Not just here in Metro City, but maybe the world" Kay said. "Yeah, yeah. Can I get some sleep now?" Rocky asked as he turned over in his basket and began snoring softly. "I guess today was pretty busy" she said as she closed her eyes and fell asleep. Meanwhile, on the outskirts of town, something strange was happening. A spaceship shaped like a baby's bottle was landing on earth. Stepping out of the huge ship was a fifty-foot baby with a huge rattle. "After traveling through the galaxy, I have finally found a planet to call my own! If anyone on this planet should challenge me, I will crush them! I will no longer simply desire to have my way, here I will have it" the Big Baby said laughing as he headed toward Metro City.

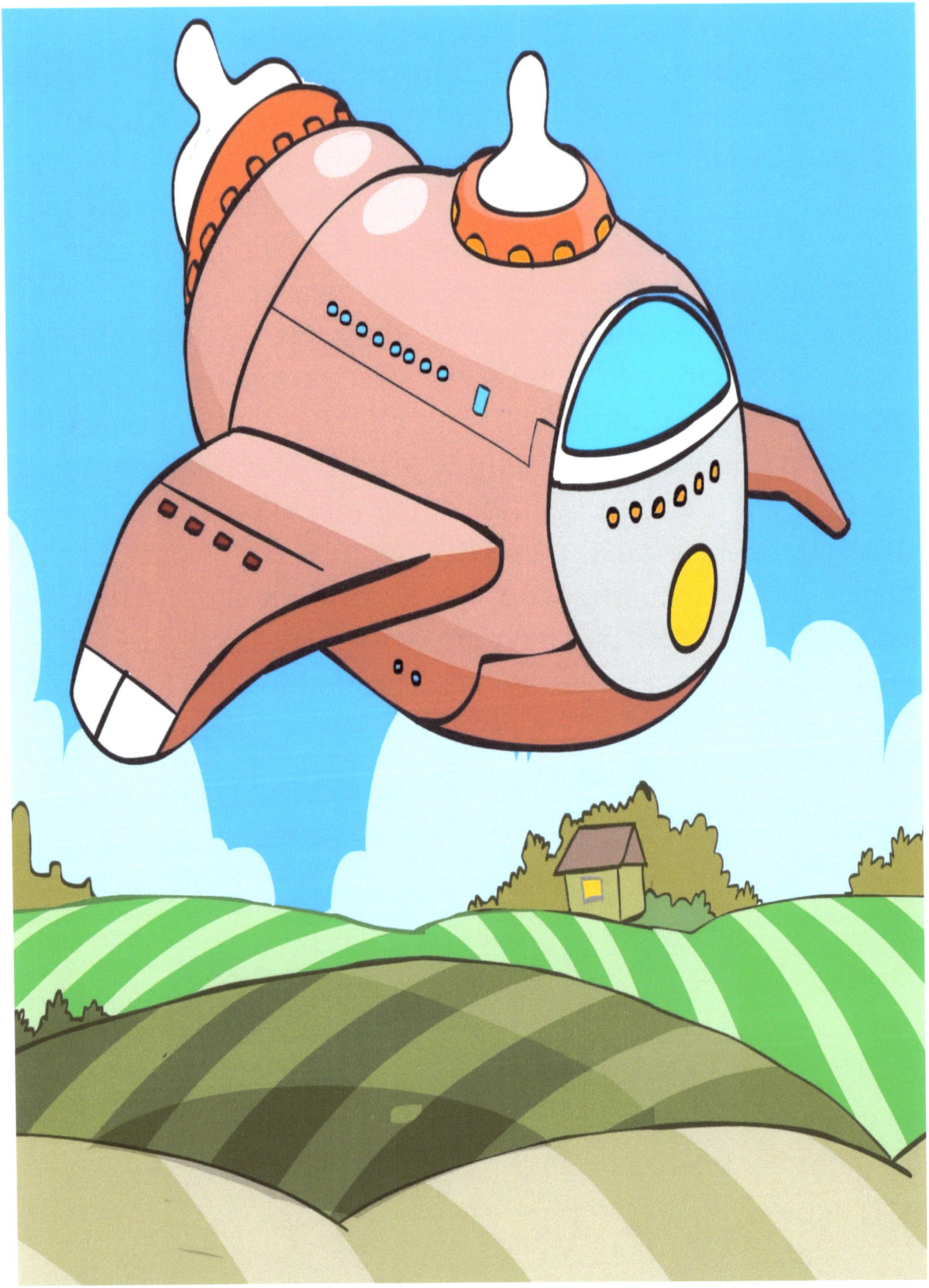

The next morning Kay and Rocky awakened to find the city in trouble once again. Looking at the television, they saw there were people without water and parts of the city on fire. "Look at that!" Rocky shouted as they saw Big Baby for the first time on the television. "Destroying your water supply and city is only the beginning. This won't end until you surrender the city to me!" Big Baby shouted at the cowering crowds. "Today you have a new leader and his name is Big Baby! You have seventy-two hours to surrender" he added as he held his huge rattle over his head and quickly vanished into thin air. Metro City was at a stand-still as its inhabitants were held captive with fear. "There must be something we can do; we can't let this go on any longer" the mayor announced to the chief of police. After twelve hours without a water supply, officials and the mayor met to discuss the problem. As they were meeting, Big Baby appeared in town square and an officer yelled "ready, aim, fire!" "You weak humans are no match for me and my atomic rattle!" Big Baby yelled as he fired an earth shaking ray toward the officers surrounding him. "Boom!" The ray shattered nearby police cars, tossing them into the air like toys. Screams of people filled the air as Big Baby used his rattle to batter buildings as he walked throughout the city. Cars crumbled beneath his huge feet as he fired rays at nearby buildings. "I want things my way and my way only!" he yelled as he stomped down the road. "I came to this planet because I never got my way on my planet and I was always the youngest and smallest in my family." So just give up because you are no match for me. My research tells me things will be different here because I'm stronger than you humans and no one can stop me!" "Think again diaper boy!" Kay interrupted his rant as she and Rocky arrived on the scene. "Who are you? My research never detected flying humans!" Big Baby said surprised. "Well I guess your research was wrong!" "Now I suggest you check that diaper you're wearing and go back to your own planet!" Rocky shouted. "No I won't it will be another two thousand years before I'm old enough to be in charge of anything on my planet!" Big Baby whined. "You will never rule Metro City." Kay shouted.

As she was speaking Big Baby fired a fire ball at her. "Look out!" Rocky shouted to Kay. Flying out of harms' way, the huge fire ball missed Kay and hit a fire truck and took out a fire hydrant below. "Why you!" Rocky shouted as he flew with super speed toward Big Baby striking him with a super paw and Big Baby swung his rattle missing him. "Is that all you got?" Rocky growled. Speeding in again, he struck Big Baby again and circled around. "Be careful Rocky!" Kay warned. This time the huge baby lined him up perfectly and hit Rocky with a freeze ray, freezing him instantly in the air. Now falling, Kay swooped in and caught her side kick before he hit the ground. "Are you okay?" she asked. When he didn't respond, Kay turned and looked at Big Baby with anger and new found determination. With a quick leap into the air, Kay flew toward the Big Baby with light speed knocking him off his feet. Shaking his head in a sitting position, he looked up as Kay struck him with a super blow. Picking up his atomic rattle the large baby shot out a rattle ray striking Kay who didn't see it coming, flipping her backward into a trash bin full of boxes. "There's no need to refuse. I'm too powerful to stop. I will take control of each city on your planet until I have total control," he said laughing.

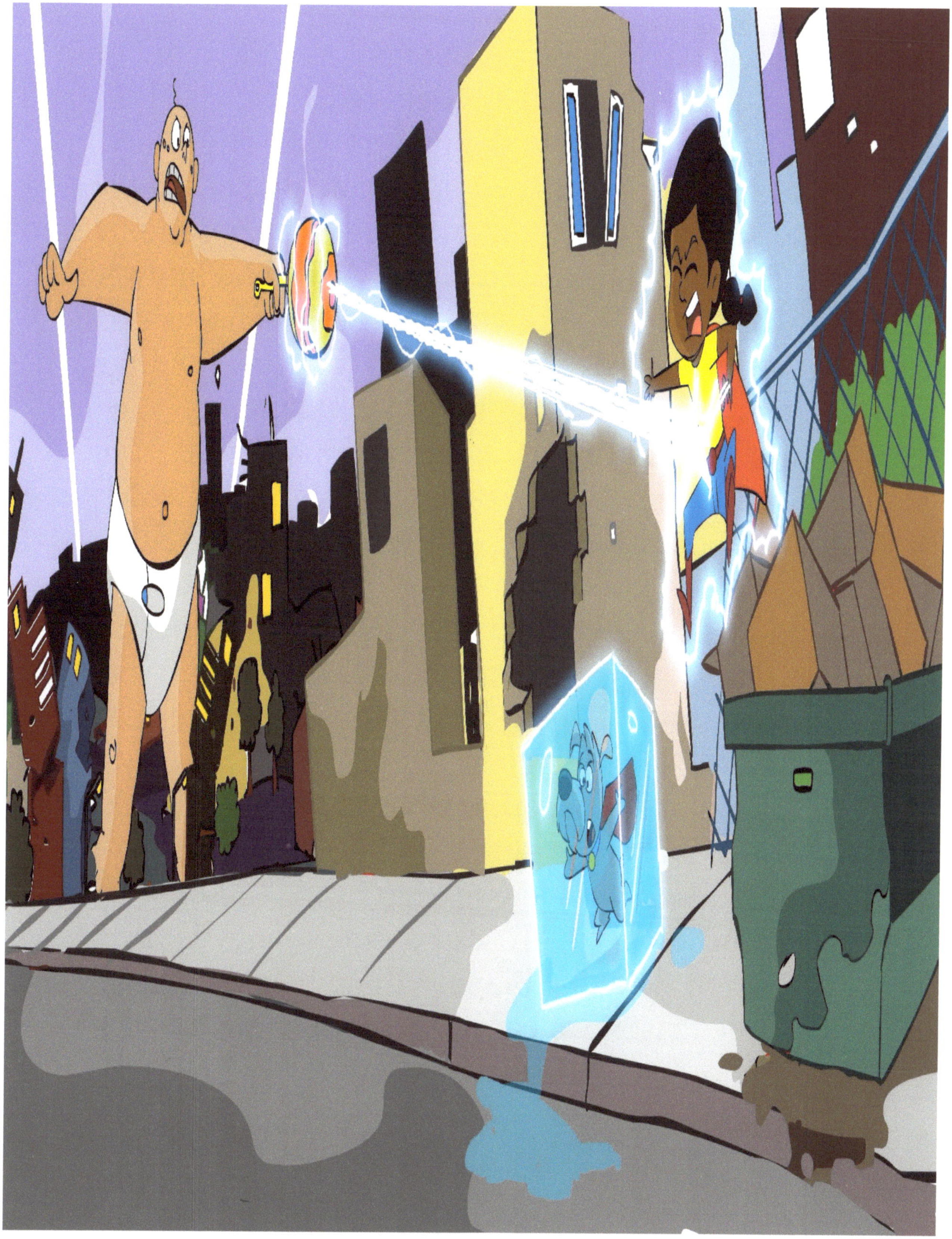

As he spoke, the officials and the mayor walked out onto the street. "Who's in charge?" demanded the Big Baby. "I am!" said Kay's dad. "I'm the mayor." As Big Baby turned and looked, he reached down and picked up the mayor and added "come with me." Looking around he said "the time is almost up to surrender." When he had spoken, he vanished again. Taking him back to his spaceship, he covered the mayor's eyes and placed him in a holding cell. "This ship is made of materials that you humans have not yet invented. It can't be detected by your simple technology." Meanwhile, climbing out of the pile of boxes, Kay looked and did not see Big Baby. She then told everyone to stand back as she used her heat ray to melt the ice around Rocky. "Are you okay Rocky?" she asked. "Yes I'm fine. Did you get him?" asked Rocky. "No I lost him and he has dad." "Lost him! How do you lose a fifty foot baby?" Rocky asked as he shook himself. Later that night at home, mom paced the floor as Kay and Rocky waited for a clue. "Some hero I am! I can't even save my own dad!" she said with tears in her eyes. "Look we will find him. I'm sure of it." Rocky assured her. "There must be a connection with that diaper villain being from another planet and the reason we can't get a signal on your dad."

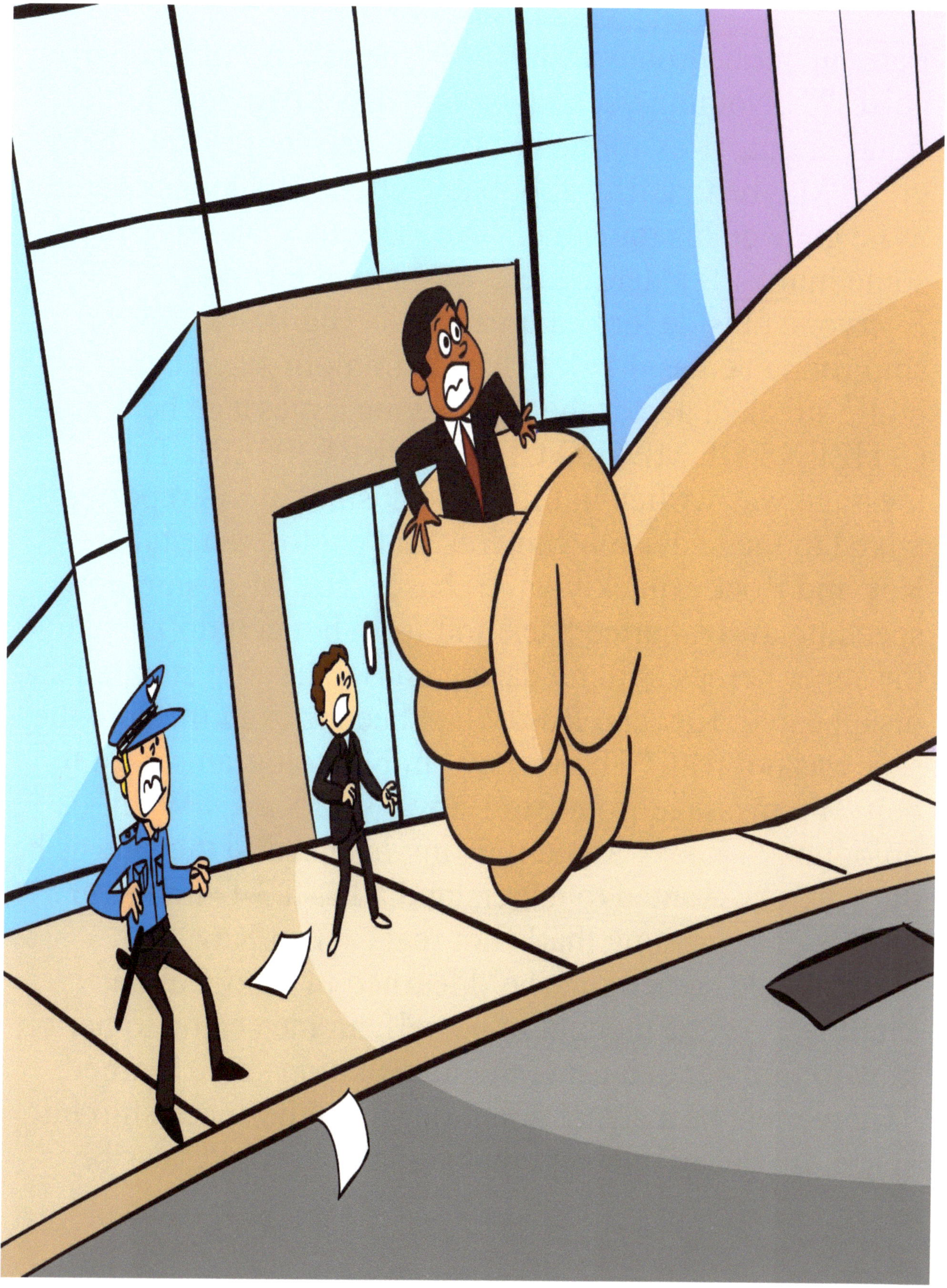

Later in her bedroom with Rocky, he asked, "any super noises?" "Nothing yet and we only have two days left to figure it out," Kay replied. "Where does a fifty-foot baby go?" "Maybe to a fifty-foot baby sitter," Rocky answered as he gnawed his toy bone. "No, seriously we have to do something!" Suddenly there was a loud b-o-o-m! Everyone outside looked up and saw Big Baby's rocket ship flying across the sky. The mammoth-sized baby bottle streaked across the sky leaving a message behind it: CITIZENS OF METRO CITY, SURRENDER! The message was written in thick, black smoke. As reporters talked to the television cameras and photos were taken, Kay and Rocky quickly gave chase. The large ship now speeding away, darted back and forth but couldn't shake the super heroes. After a daring chase, the ship stopped and disappeared. Kay and Rocky had been tricked the ship they saw was not real. "These were simply holograms used to deliver a message from Big Baby," said Kay. "What's a hologram?" Rocky asked twisting his head to the side as he did when he wanted to understand. "It's a 3-D image or picture of something that's not real." Then Kay remembered something she'd learned in school about satellites. As she thought to herself, an idea came to her on how to find her dad using the information she'd learned. "There must be a signal going out from the space ship into space. If we can intercept that signal, we could possibly find where he's located." Kay explained. "Hey that's not a bad idea," an excited Rocky said.

Flying through the sky searching for a space signal. Suddenly Kay started getting strange vibrations and asked "do you feel that Rocky?" "You mean those strange radio wave vibrations?" "Yes, we must be getting closer to the spot." Kay answered. They were suddenly caught in a strange magnetic force which pulled them closer to the earth. As they were being held in midair, far from town, a voice spoke from below them. "I knew you would come looking for me after seeing the holograms" said the whiny voice. "It's that Dr. Diaper baby guy" Rocky said as he squirmed to break free. "That's Big Baby you miserable flea bag!" Big Baby yelled. "There's no use in trying to break free. I've studied your chemical makeup and found you to be electrically charged with a force which magnetizes you to my ship." "He's right. It's no use, Rocky, I can't move. We're in trouble!" "That's right you are in trouble and soon you two will bow down to me – Big Baby!" Soon they found themselves magnetized to the inside of the vessel stretched across the ceiling of the ship. Looking around, it seemed like a combination of a baby's room and something out of a science fiction movie. Kay spotted her dad. He was blindfolded and tied down. "Hello! Is there someone there? Hello?" her dad said. When Kay realized Big Baby was gone she answered "yes there is" changing her voice slightly. "Who are you? How did you get here? Where are we?" Her dad asked one question after the next. "Look, we are here to help you. Just relax and stay calm" Kay said. "What now? Because I'm not relaxed or calm either" Rocky chimed. "There must be a way to shut off the magnetic force" Kay said as she glanced around the room. Then she spotted a large red button on a far wall. With an intense stare, Kay's heat ray began to work. The rays from her eyes soon began to melt the area around the button and without warning, they were hurtling towards the floor of the ship. The magnetic force of the ship had been disabled. "Hello. What's going on?" Kay's dad spoke up. "Nothing sir, just stay calm" Kay answered. "Nothing indeed sir!" a voice echoed from a huge doorway. It was Big Baby. "Looking to escape? Maybe you should think again. All exits are sealed and my baby clones will detain you." "Baby clones? What's a baby clone?" Rocky asked. With a motion of his huge rattle, Big Baby summoned a large army of robotic babies. "Okay. I'm sorry I asked" Rocky said. Now backed into a corner, Kay and Rocky began defending themselves against the army of miniature robotic babies.

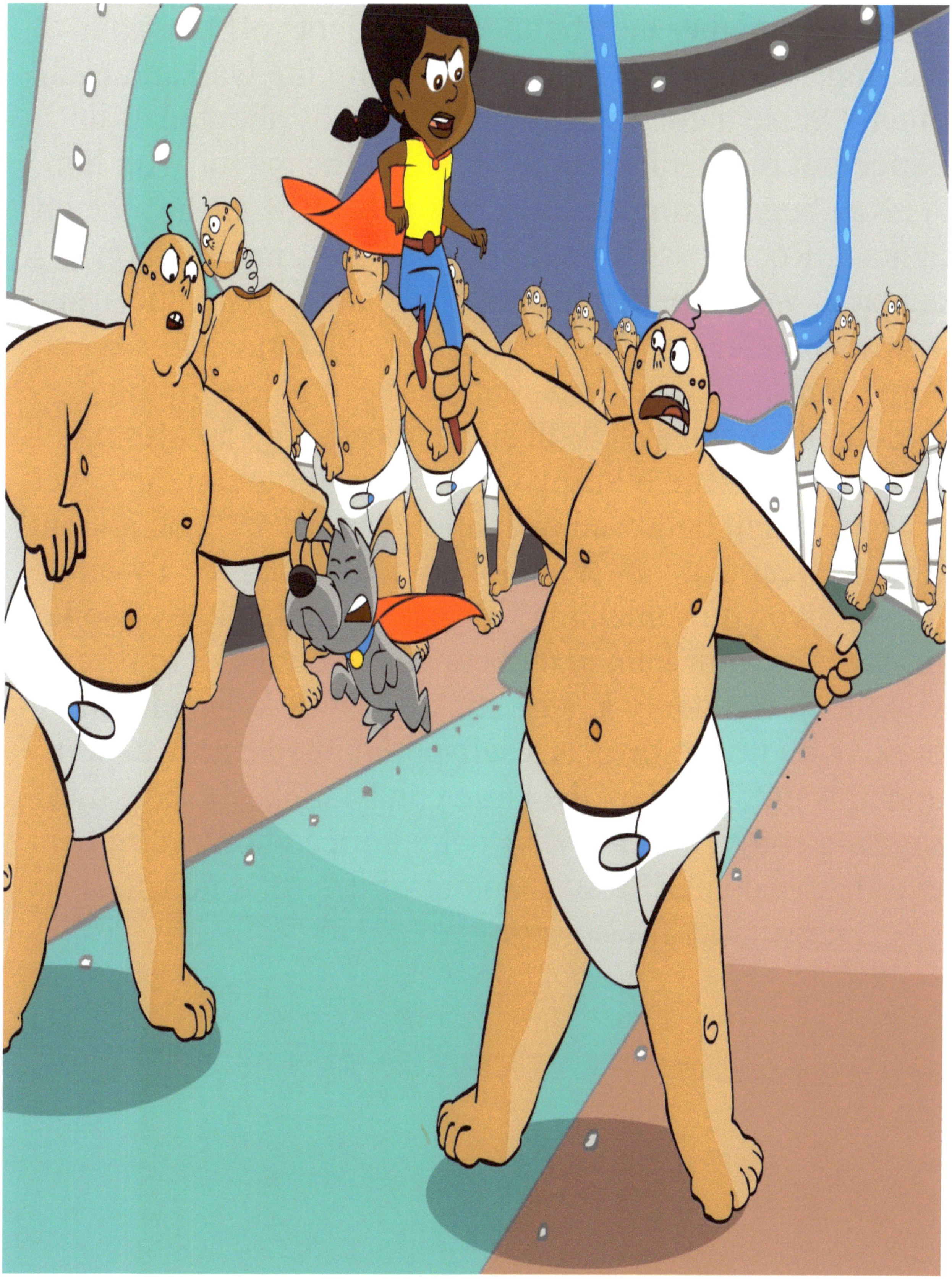

One after another they bounced the robots off the walls of the ship. Each one exploded as they hit the wall and each other. "Seize them, seize them" Big Baby shouted as he darted out of the huge room and took the mayor with him. As Kay began using her heat ray to explode each robot on contact, Rocky was blowing cold air freezing them on contact. With a punch here and a heat ray there, the army was soon defeated. Now flying through large hallways, Kay soon spotted her dad. He had been placed in the middle of a hallway. With super speed, Kay and Rocky were off to rescue him. Just before reaching him, however, a whiny laugh bellowed over a loud speaker. "You are but a small weak human. You are no match for me. I would like to give you something" Big Baby said. "I have done research on your human makeup and would like to offer you this." Suddenly a huge stick of candy was before her eyes. Kay was known as a self-proclaimed candy expert and now entranced by the large candy stick, she began to say "c-a-n-d-y, c-a-n-d-y!" Rocky noticed how weird her eyes had become. "Kay snap out of it." "It's no use. She's now under my control.

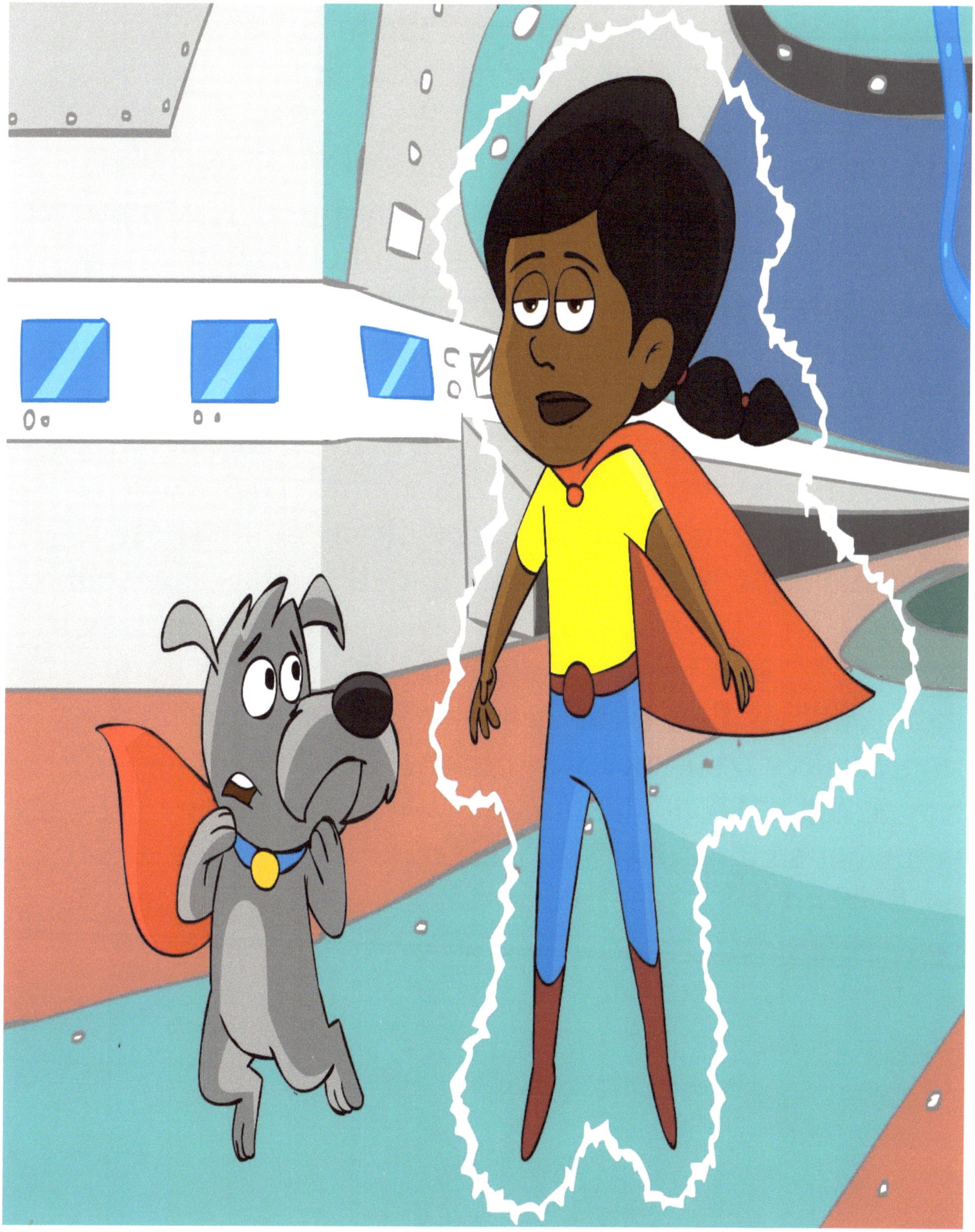

You too will now feel my wrath" the huge baby villain yelled as he pointed his huge rattle toward Rocky. "Seize him!" he ordered Kay to capture Rocky. "Hey now wait a minute. Kay, it's me your old pal Rocky" he explained as he backed up slowly. "C-a-n-d-y, c-a-n-d-y" Kay muttered as she blasted a heat ray in his direction. "Hey that was close. What are you doing? I thought we were partners!" Kay suddenly tackled him and took him by his ears, flying to the top of the ship. With a burst of speed of his own, Rocky began to fly wildly, leaving a dizzy Kay holding on like a roller coaster ride. Zip-zap-zoom! The two were entangled as if in a rodeo. Rocky, flying at top speed as Kay held on to his ears, quickly darted right as she went left smashing her into the ship's wall. He grabbed Kay by her pant leg and began flying in small circular motions then suddenly flew right through the huge candy stick. Immediately the trance was broken. "What's going on?" Kay asked. "What's going on? What's going on? I'll tell you what's going on! You tried to turn me into a H-o-t D-o-g!" "Hot dog? What are you talking about?" Kay was confused.

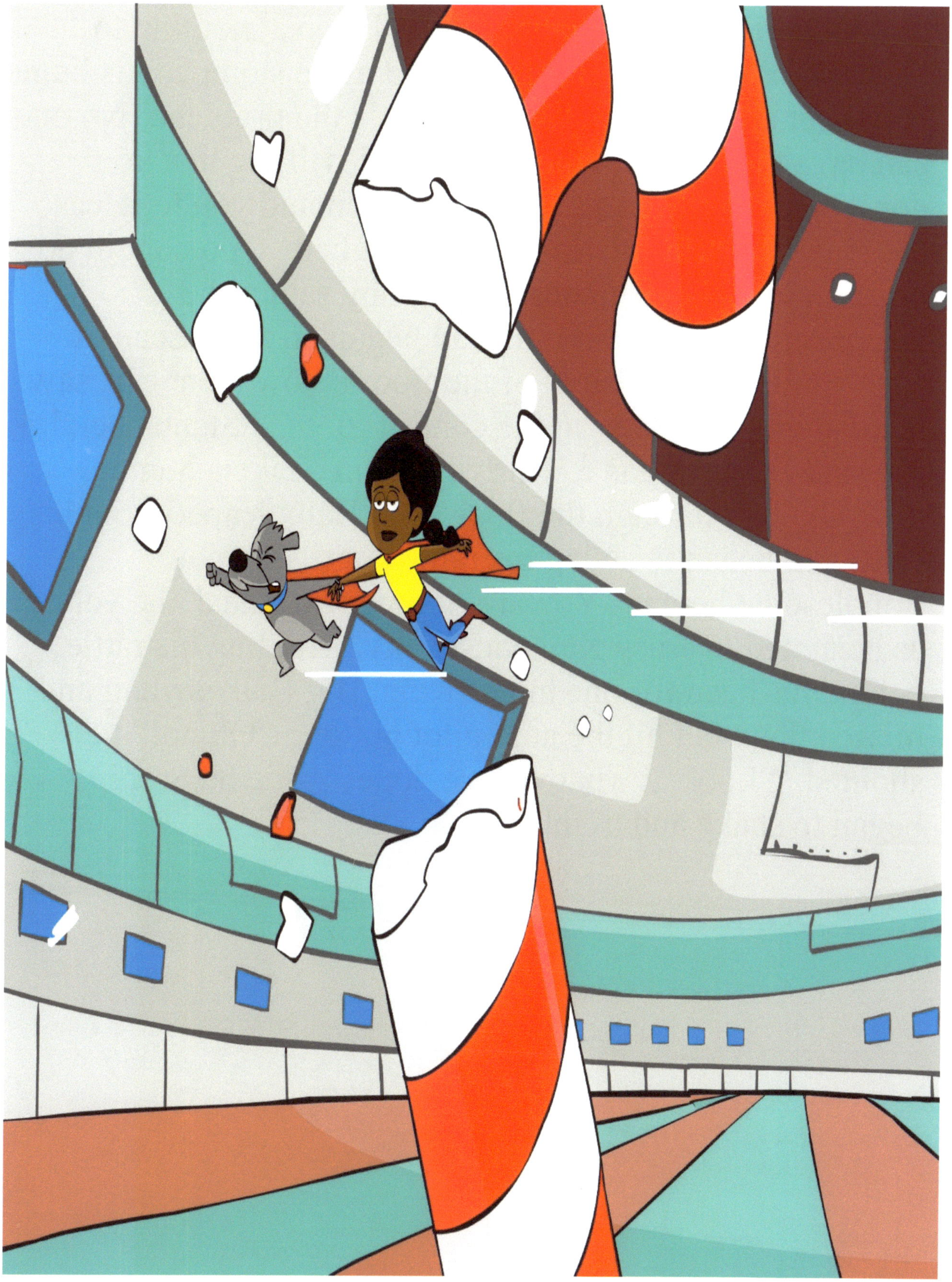

"Enough of this jibber jabber. I will stop at nothing to have my own way!" Big Baby said as he stomped his huge baby feet on the floor. "Maybe that's the problem. No one can have their way all the time! But I will see that you don't take over Metro City. Now I demand you to release the mayor!" "Ha-ha, Ha-ha!" he laughed. "You are in no position to make demands!" Big Baby said as he disappeared from the room. Kay began an x-ray scan of each wall. With a search of the floor below them, she saw her dad and Big Baby in the control room. "Stand back" she said as she began a whirlwind spin. Like a human drill, she was through the floor. Big Baby leaped from his chair and began to swing his rattle angrily. "You troublesome human! You are ruining my plans!" he yelled as he aimed to crush Kay and Rocky. Holding his rattle behind his head for one huge swing, Big Baby swung and missed them but hit the auto pilot button. "Oh no!" he shouted. "Look at what you've done!" The huge ship began to shake and tremble.

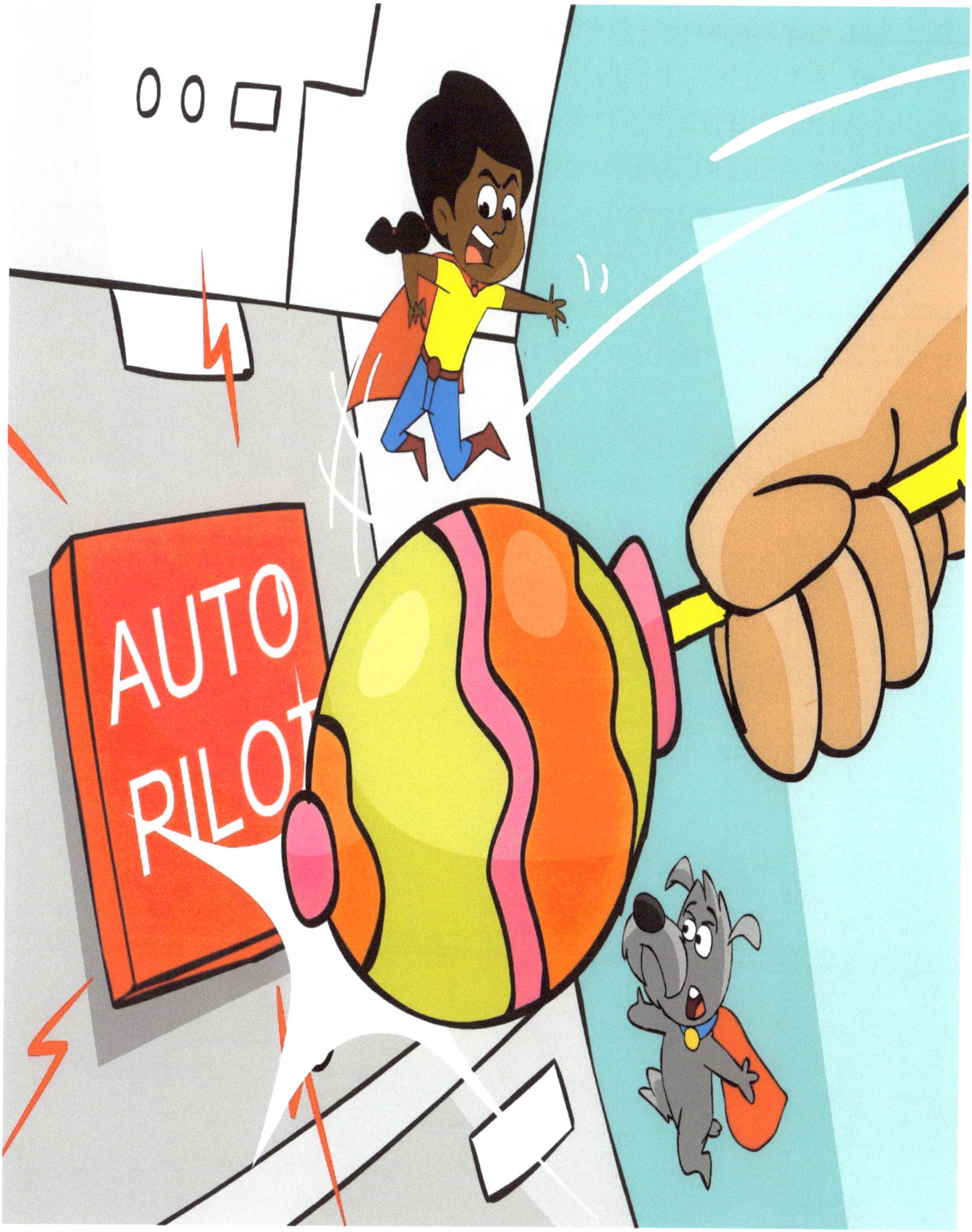
AUTO
RILOT

The ship now started Kay had to think quickly, "Rocky, take the mayor to safety and I will handle the rest." Rocky grabbed the mayor and got him out of the ship to safety. "How dare you stop my plans like this!" he cried. Then Big Baby did something Kay didn't expect. He began to cry and pound the floor with his fist. "It's not fair, it's not fair! I want to have my way!" he whined. While he wasn't looking, Kay quickly took his huge rattle and broke it into pieces.

"What are you doing?" Big Baby yelled. "That was a one of a kind rattle!" he shouted and charged at Kay to try and crush her. But with one quick side step to the left, she caused him to trip and land face-first onto the floor. Attempting to get up, she took him by his leg and spun him around until he was dizzy. Then restrained him to the control seat of the aircraft by using her heat ray to melt metal around his wrists. "What are you doing?" "I'm setting your auto pilot back to your home and sending you back through space. "Wait! You can't! I mean don't!!!" Big Baby whined. With the ship now taking off, Kay rushed to exit in time. As the ship left the earth's surface, Big Baby could still be heard whining loudly. Just before the ship left earth's view he yelled "I'll be back! I'll be back!!!"

Kay and Rocky took the mayor home, rang the doorbell and left him alone on the porch. When her mother noticed her husband at the front door, she set him free and removed his blindfold. Once inside, he kissed his wife, holding her for a long while. Later, he went upstairs to check on Kay and found her sound asleep in her bed with Rocky laying quietly at her feet. After kissing her head and petting Rocky, he decided to surprise her in the morning and slowly left the room. Kay and Rocky both opened their eyes. "You think he has a clue?" Rocky asked. "Nope. He'll never know" she answered and smiled as she closed her eyes.

For more information on

The Adventures of Superkay and Rocky

Visit

Superkayandrocky.com

Also available on Amazon books.com and kindle

www.ingramcontent.com/pod-product-compliance
Lightning Source LLC
Chambersburg PA
CBHW042127040426
42450CB00002B/102